Project 1
Brain Breakthrough

PROJECT 1 - BRAIN BREAKTHROUGH
iT'S THE BRAIN BUSTER!

PLTS objective: To understand the power and flexibility of the brain and how it can be developed using the competences.

GET EXCITED!

Consider this headline: 'Scientists discover that the brain has amazing undiscovered powers'. What could they be?

....

....

....

....

....

FACTS

Your brain has 100 billion neurons (brain cells).

You learn by making connections between neurons.

Your brain is more powerful than a computer the size of Wembley Stadium.

MAIN ACTIVITY

What undiscovered powers could your brain have?

....

....

What brain power would help you with learning?

....

....

4

iT'S THE BRAIN BUSTER!...
- CONTiNUED

PLTS objective: To understand the power and flexibility of the brain and how it can be developed using the competences.

Growing your competences (a cluster of skills and abilities) will help you be a successful learner. What skills and abilities would you like to develop to make you a great learner?

....

....

Competence	Impact	Saying
Self-discipline Listening Optimism	Get things done	No pain, no gain

Look at the PLTS and decide how good you are at each of these.

Think of a famous person that might be a top scorer for each of the PLTS.

....

Create a PLTS card for your bedside table. Use the sayings and create cartoon pictures to help you remember the PLTS.

WHERE ARE YOU GOING?

PLTS objective: Being able to set goals and think ahead.

GET EXCITED!

What would you do if you won £100,000 pounds?
What is your dream job of the future? Just
imagining this sparks off neurons because having
a dream or goal produces the chemicals that drive
you to succeed.

MAIN ACTIVITY

'Where are you going?' said the rabbit to Alice. 'I don't know,' said Alice.

'Well, you will never get there then,' sneered the rabbit.

Create a story about a successful footballer or pop star. Imagine you know how
they got where they are today. Write the story of their lives in a paragraph.
Share your stories. As well as their skills, what themes did all your stories have in
common?

....

....

....

....

Most successful people had goals and
dreams long before they made it big.
How did they do it?

1. They had a goal.

2. They believed they could
   achieve it.

3. They used strategies that
   worked to achieve their
   goals.

WHERE ARE YOU GOING?
- CONTINUED

PLTS objective: Being able to set goals and think ahead.

If *they* can do it, *you* can do it ... but first you have to set yourself short-term and long-term goals and think about how you will set about achieving them.

My long-term goal/dream is ....

....

I will achieve this by ....

....

Today I will ....

....

The time to start working towards your goals is *now*. Simply by writing down and committing to a goal you make a new and important connection in the brain. A part of the brain lights up whenever a challenge or goal is created.

Create three important goals for this year:

1. ....

....

2. ....

....

3. ....

....

PROJECT 1 – BRAIN BREAKTHROUGH
WHERE ARE YOU GOING?
– CONTINUED

PLTS objective: Being able to set goals and think ahead.

Create two personal goals for the next five years:

1. ....

....

2. ....

....

It is five years from now. Describe a day in your life in the present tense.

....

....

....

....

Task: Interview your partner as a 30-year-old, talking about their school life and how they achieved their amazing success.

Extension task: At home, research into the lives of your heroes and how they achieved success.

HOW DID I DO?

How can the competencies help you achieve your goals? Write a headline in a local newspaper about your amazing achievements.

....

....

....

....

PROJECT 1 – BRAIN BREAKTHROUGH

MAKE THE TEAM

PLTS objective: Developing teamwork skills.

ACTIVITY
3
PROJECT 1   1 HOUR

GET EXCITED!

How do you learn best? Munching? Drinking? Sitting up? Lying down? With friends? With music on? We all have different needs, so how can we make your classroom good for you?

MAIN ACTIVITY

PLTS lessons are about teamwork and independent learning but how can we make sure the learning environment is good for everyone? Take a vote on it! If we all agree and understand the rules then we all feel safe and happy. This is the democratic approach.

Democratic values are important for your learning environment. What does democracy mean? Think of three words that sum up democracy for you.

1. ....

2. ....

3. ....

Make a list of everything you have ever voted for—from television shows to school elections.

....

....

....

....

....

Values for life include love, loyalty, friendship, money, fun … What are your top three values?

1. ....

2. ....

3. ....

You vote according to your values. Values are what you believe to be important in life. They help you make good rules.

MAKE THE TEAM - CONTINUED

PLTS objective: Developing teamwork skills.

Now make a set of five rules for your teamwork activities. Get into teams of five. Now look at each others' rules. Vote on your favourite rules for the team. What should be the five rules for your teamwork?

1. ....

2. ....

3. ....

4. ....

5. ....

Now prepare a manifesto for your team. This should include:

• Team name ....

• Team shield with visual representations of each rule.

PROJECT 1 - BRAIN BREAKTHROUGH
MAKE THE TEAM - CONTINUED

PLTS objective: Developing teamwork skills.

- Five team rules and why you have chosen them (this may be linked to your values).

1. ....

2. ....

3. ....

4. ....

5. ....

- A speech you can deliver to the class that explains all about your team.

....

....

....

....

....

....

....

....

HOW DID I DO?

How did you work as a team?

....

....

Who had the best set of rules?

....

....

BUILDING BRILLIANT COMMUNICATION SKILLS

ACTIVITY 4
PROJECT 1 2 HOURS

PLTS objective: To become a great communicator so that you work well with others.

GET EXCITED!

Listen to the sounds around you now – jot down everything you can hear. Now listen to your insides—what can you hear? Listening also requires you to look at *body language* to understand what someone is really saying. Look around the room and see what bodies are saying to you. Are they happy, focused or fidgety?

MAIN ACTIVITY

Some people learn well when they are listening. This is a very important skill to acquire as so much of what we have to learn requires *good listening skills*.

How do you know you have heard something? What mental processes go on after you have heard something important?

1. In pairs, find out how good you are at listening. Here are some activities that will involve careful listening: Tell your partner some details of your last holiday—make them repeat back to you the main points.

2. Now tell each other a story about what you did last weekend—without words, just actions.

3. Show the following emotions through your facial expressions: happiness, anger, sadness, not understanding, curiosity.

If you can learn to read body language then you will start to gain *rapport*, which is a French word for brilliant communication. To get good rapport you need good eye contact, a slight head tilt and to mirror and match the person you are listening to. Try not to block by folding your arms, look away or stare too much, or turn your body away.

TASK 1

(In threes with one observer) imagine you are at a counselling session. One of you is the counsellor, one the client. Tell the counsellor your real (or imaginary) problems about school or home in three or four minutes. The counsellor then has to repeat back to you a summary of the problems and suggest some solutions. The observer reports back on how good the listening was.

Now swap and this time the listener has to use body language to encourage the client. The observer can now report on the listening and the body language and demonstrate the best to the class.

BUILDING BRILLIANT COMMUNICATION SKILLS - CONTINUED

ACTIVITY
4
PROJECT 1 PAGE 2

PLTS objective: To become a great communicator so that you work well with others.

TASK 2

Try listening to your internal dialogue—the voice that talks to you inside your head. It often gives you a running commentary on what you are doing and what you are going to do. What sort of voice is it? Is it your voice? Try to make it positive and encouraging. This can be very motivating.

Look at this example: You are asked to do a bungee jump for charity. There are two thoughts that may come into your head. Your negative voice says, 'I might die! People get injured. I might chicken out at the last minute and look like a fool.' Your positive voice says, 'That could be exciting. I can do it and think how good it would make me feel. I will be making money for someone else.' Which voice would you have?

Now practice making your internal voice say something positive to you. Make the most of self-talk to build your confidence and self-belief.

AVOID – Negative self-talk	INCREASE – Positive self-talk
I can't do it	I'm brilliant and beautiful!
She hates me	I can do anything if I work hard enough
I've never been good at exams	I love exams
My writing is rubbish	I am an excellent friend
No one likes me	I am very determined to get it right
It's bound to go wrong	I am born lucky
Add some more …	*Add some more …*
....	....
....	....
....	....
....	....
....	....

Mind–body connection. Say each of the positive statements above and practice putting the body language with it—it's much more powerful.

BUILDiNG BRiLLiANT COMMUNiCATiON SKiLLS - CONTiNUED

ACTIVITY
4
PROJECT 1 PAGE 3

PLTS objective: To become a great communicator so that you work well with others.

TASK 3

Stand back-to-back with a partner and show the two voices—positive and negative—as you are asked these questions by a third person: Do you want to come to my party? Have you done your homework? Can you wash the dishes, please? Do you fancy me?

Tips for great communication:

• Listen with your ears and your body.

• Smile and nod.

• Tune in to any feedback your audience is giving you.

• Be present—don't think of other things.

• Keep good eye contact.

• Be enthusiastic and excited about what you are saying.

• Be clear and precise.

• Use gestures to help you.

HOW DiD i DO?

Finish these sentences:

A good listener always...

I can get good rapport by..

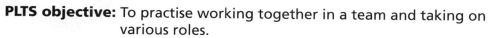

PROJECT 1 - BRAIN BREAKTHROUGH
TEAMWORK - TOGETHER EVERYONE ACHIEVES MORE

ACTIVITY 5 · PROJECT 1 · 1 HOUR

PLTS objective: To practise working together in a team and taking on various roles.

MAIN ACTIVITY

GET EXCITED!

Think of the best teams you know. Why do they succeed?

Form your team, allocate the following roles and make a note of them:

- *Team leader* – leads the whole team and makes the final decisions for the group, often presenting ideas back to the class.

- *Timekeeper* – reminds the team how much time they have left and makes sure all the jobs get done.

- *Notetaker* – keeps notes of all information and decisions.

- *Includer* – makes sure everyone has a chance to speak and have their opinions heard.

- *Listener* – makes sure everyone in the team is listening to each other and also not making too much noise and disturbing other groups.

TASK

As a team your task is to create your own country. You have some paper and pens and one hour to create a national identity for your country. You will need to present your country to the whole class.

HOW DID I DO?

Rate yourself out of ten as a member of the group.

....

Rate each other out of ten in their roles.

....

Share your scores and discuss how you can improve.

PiCTURE THiS - MAKiNG LEARNiNG MAPS

ACTIVITY
6
PROJECT 1 · 1 HOUR

PLTS objective: To develop your self-awareness and creativity as a learner.

GET EXCiTED!

Use your eyes to see and use your brain to create visual pictures. Imagine a frog sitting on your table. What colour is it? Touch it and feel its slimy skin. Now try a cat—hear it purring. If you find it hard to visualise these animals, it could be hard for you to use internal visualising for learning so you need to practise!

Here are two powerful learning tools to help you make the most of your visual learning.

MAiN ACTiViTY

Creating a learning map involves using all the important information you need to know but writing it down in a way that is brain-friendly and captures your visual imagination. Most of the time we write our notes in lists and paragraphs. This does not always help us remember them.

Good learning maps use colour, images, symbols and words. These are all brain-friendly and stimulate us visually. They start with a central idea and grow branches in all directions as ideas flow. It doesn't matter if they are not artistic or organised.

PICTURE THIS - MAKING LEARNING MAPS - CONTINUED

ACTIVITY
6
PROJECT 1   PAGE 2

PLTS objective: To develop your self-awareness and creativity as a learner.

MY FAVOURITE SUBJECT

Take your favourite subject and create a learning map of everything you know about it. Put the main themes on the trunk and branches and all the other ideas on the little twigs that come from them. It doesn't matter if it is untidy or not logical as long as you understand it—just get as much down as you can. Now add lots of pictures and symbols to make it more interesting and memorable.

Give it to a neighbour to study for five minutes—then test how much they have learnt about that subject. Ask them how they remembered bits of the map. Was it through the pictures or the words? Did they see the map inside their heads? If they did they were using their visual memory.

PiCTURE THiS - MAKiNG LEARNiNG MAPS - CONTiNUED

ACTIVITY
6
PROJECT 1   PAGE 3

PLTS objective: To develop your self-awareness and creativity as a learner.

MY DiFFiCULT SUBJECT

Now try creating a learning map for another subject you find more difficult or for a book you are studying—don't forget to use lots of colour and pictures.

MULTIPLE INTELLIGENCES - THERE ARE LOTS OF WAYS TO BE CLEVER!

ACTIVITY
7
PROJECT 1   1 HOUR

PLTS objective: Develop self-awareness about how learning works for you.

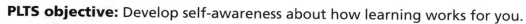

GET EXCITED!

TASK 1: HOW MANY WAYS AM I CLEVER?

Find out in this section how you are intelligent in many different ways and how you can use this to improve your learning.

Write a list of three things you are good at and say why. Is it the same to be clever at playing football and clever at Maths? Are you clever if you can make plants grow or draw fantastic pictures? Discuss what it means to be clever.

Neuroscientists now think that intelligence isn't just being good at Maths or English but there are many different ways to be intelligent. You have *multiple intelligences*. There are lots of ways you are smart—here are some of them:

- Interpersonal – people smart
- Logical – number smart
- Artisitc – picture smart
- Musical – music smart

- Intrapersonal – self smart
- Linguistic – word smart
- Kinesthetic/physical – body smart
- Naturalist – nature smart

Discuss each one with a friend and then fill in the box to rate yourself on each of the Smarts.

People smart

Are you good at getting on with people—not just your friends but adults, children, teachers? Are you a good listener, showing consideration and tolerance?

How do I rate myself?

*1 (rubbish)*_____*10 (brilliant)*

Explain how/why you decided:

....

....

MULTIPLE INTELLIGENCES – THERE ARE LOTS OF WAYS TO BE CLEVER! – CONTINUED

ACTIVITY
7
PROJECT 1 PAGE 2

PLTS objective: Develop self-awareness about how learning works for you.

Self smart

Understanding yourself and the way you work is vital for success in life. Can you control your moods and motivate yourself? Can you explain the way you behave in certain situations? Are you good at setting yourself targets and sticking to promises?

How do I rate myself?

*1 (rubbish)*_____*10 (brilliant)*

Explain how/why you decided:

....

....

Word smart

If you enjoy reading and talking using a well-developed vocabulary you will be word smart. You may be good at writing essays and stories and enjoy playing around with words and meanings. Your favourite lesson may be English if you are word smart.

How do I rate myself?

*1 (rubbish)*_____*10 (brilliant)*

Explain how/why you decided:

....

....

Number smart

Are you good at solving problems and sorting things out in a step-by-step fashion? Do you make lists of things to do and work through them? Your favourite subjects may be Maths and Science and you enjoy brainteasers and puzzles. If this sounds like you, you are number smart.

How do I rate myself?

*1 (rubbish)*_____*10 (brilliant)*

Explain how/why you decided:

....

....

20

PROJECT 1 - BRAIN BREAKTHROUGH
MULTIPLE INTELLIGENCES - THERE ARE LOTS OF WAYS TO BE CLEVER! - CONTINUED

ACTIVITY 7
PROJECT 1 PAGE 3

PLTS objective: Develop self-awareness about how learning works for you.

Picture smart

Do you think in pictures? If you enjoy drawing, painting and looking at pictures, these are signs of visual/spatial intelligence. Learning more effectively from maps, graphs and pictures is easy for picture smart people.

How do I rate myself?

1 (rubbish)_____10 (brilliant)

Explain how/why you decided:

....

....

Body smart

This is the ability to use your body skilfully in sport, dance or in building and constructing things. If you are strong in this intelligence you will enjoy lessons like PE, Drama and Technology. You will enjoy doing things yourself rather than watching others and sometimes find it hard to sit still!

How do I rate myself?

1 (rubbish)_____10 (brilliant)

Explain how/why you decided:

....

....

Music smart

If you have got good rhythm and enjoy singing or playing an instrument you are likely to have a strong musical intelligence. Do you listen to a variety of music because you want to and can you pick out patterns and instruments that others don't seem to notice? This is another sign of being music smart.

How do I rate myself?

1 (rubbish)_____10 (brilliant)

Explain how/why you decided:

....

....

21

MULTIPLE INTELLIGENCES - THERE ARE LOTS OF WAYS TO BE CLEVER! - CONTINUED

PLTS objective: Develop self-awareness about how learning works for you.

Nature smart

If you are nature smart then you are aware and interested in plants and animals, and the environment. You may love being outdoors and care about the environment around you. You may be very aware of animal rights issues and hope to have a career in an outdoor environment.

How do I rate myself?

*1 (rubbish)*_____*10 (brilliant)*

Explain how/why you decided:

....

....

TASK 2

Think of a time when you used each intelligence. Do you use some more than others? Write down which you have used and when.

....

....

....

....

....

HOW DID I DO?

In groups create a school visit that uses *all* the intelligences. Write your schedule for the day.

....

....

....

....

....

EMOTIONAL INTELLIGENCE (1) - TAKE CONTROL OF YOUR MOODS!

ACTIVITY
8
PROJECT 1   1 HOUR

PLTS objective: To take control of your thinking and create positive outcomes.

GET EXCITED!

What mood are you in? What puts you in a good/bad mood? Circle on this scale where you think you are:

Despairing … depressed … a bit down … OK … quite good … good … very good … ecstatic

Explain to your neighbour how you know and why you feel like this.

MAIN ACTIVITY

The mood you are in can change the outcome of events—if you can control your moods then you can control your life. What puts you in a bad mood or a good mood? Make a list with two columns.

Your facial expression and your posture are very influenced by your mood. How can you tell what mood someone is in? Fill in this chart to show how body language is affected by mood.

Mood	Signs
Happy	Smiling, sitting up, active, alert
Angry	....
Sad	....
Anxious	....
_____	....
_____	....
_____	....
_____	....
_____	....
_____	....
_____	....

PLTS objective: To take control of your thinking and create positive
outcomes.

Mind–body connection

Laugh loudly *now*—just by physically laughing endorphins are triggered that make you feel good.

It is impossible to be in a bad mood if you hold your head up, put your shoulders back and walk with a bounce in your step—try it!

TASK

It is Monday morning breakfast time. Act out the typical scene. Then change the mood of each of the actors to see how it changes the scene.

Your mood has the power to influence others—bad moods are contagious, good moods are infectious and spread happiness.

Create a mood monitor for your bedroom—use card to cut out and make the mood monitor. Write on the different moods and use a paper clip to show your current mood. When you have completed this and shown your own mood, work in pairs to try to change each others' mood.

EMOTIONAL INTELLIGENCE (1) – TAKE CONTROL OF YOUR MOODS! – CONTINUED

PLTS objective: To take control of your thinking and create positive outcomes.

How can we change our own mood? Write down three ways:

1. ....

2. ....

3. ....

How can we change each other's moods? Write down three ways:

1. ....

2. ....

3. ....

HOW DID I DO?

Who decides what mood you are in?

....

EMOTIONAL INTELLIGENCE (2) - SELF-BELIEF AND SOWING SEEDS OF OPTIMISM

ACTIVITY
9
PROJECT 1   2 HOURS

PLTS objective: Develop a confident approach to challenges.

GET EXCITED!

Consider: if you think you can or if you think you can't, you are right. Believe in yourself and your skills and abilities. You can be your own worst enemy if you don't believe in yourself. What happens to people who don't believe in themselves?

MAIN ACTIVITY

Think about how we try to predict our future using horoscopes.

Today be very careful because everything is set to work against you. Mistakes will turn into disasters and expect to have an argument with someone you really care about. Mars is ascending in your orbit and that means you are susceptible to losing it big time. Watch out! How will this change your behaviour?

Today you will have a great day and meet someone special. Everyone will want to help you out and finally appreciate your skills. The moon in Jupiter means your luck is endless today so expect to come into some money! How will this affect your behaviour?

Write a typical horoscope entry for this week to yourself.

....

....

....

....

....

....

....

....

EMOTIONAL INTELLIGENCE (2) – SELF-BELIEF AND SOWING SEEDS OF OPTIMISM – CONTINUED

PLTS objective: Develop a confident approach to challenges.

Draw a timeline for your life from birth until now with all the main events.

Now carry it on to 2050 and put in expected events. You have just predicted your future!

EMOTIONAL INTELLIGENCE (2) - SELF-BELIEF AND SOWING SEEDS OF OPTIMISM - CONTINUED

PLTS objective: Develop a confident approach to challenges.

SEEING IS BELIEVING ...

Create a visual picture in your mind of yourself at your most brilliant. Describe it to your group. Think of a saying that will remind you of it any time you need it. For example, 'Strong and indestructible' or 'Brilliant and beautiful'. Keep saying it over and over to yourself when you think of this picture.

Now create a superhero figure that can represent you when you are feeling that good. Draw it as a cartoon figure and draw a speech bubble with the saying in it too. Stick all of your group's characters onto a piece of large card and present your Power Team to the class.

HOW DID I DO?

What do we mean by self-belief?

....

....

....

PROJECT 1 - BRAIN BREAKTHROUGH
WHAT SORT OF THINKER ARE YOU?

ACTIVITY 10 PROJECT 1 1 HOUR

PLTS objective: To extend your thinking and develop metacognition.

GET EXCITED!

What sort of thinker are you? Are you more of a creative or logical thinker? We know that we can be clever in many ways, but what about the way we think when we are learning. If you had a jigsaw puzzle to do what would you do first? What do you do when you have a new computer or mobile phone—read the instructions or try it out until you get it right?

MAIN ACTIVITY

If you can make the logical and creative parts of your brain work well together when they need to then that makes your brain very powerful.

Tick some of these that you like:

Logical	Creative
Writing	Ideas
Logic	Intuition
Numbers	Daydreams
Analysing	Sport
Reading	Playing music
Sequencing	The big picture
Language	Rhythm
Detail	Colour
Spelling	Imagination

These two halves need to work together to make our brains work really well. For example, when we are doing a jigsaw puzzle we sort out the pieces using colour and shape but we have to think about the 'big picture' and imagine how it all fits together to get it right.

WHAT SORT OF THINKER ARE YOU? – CONTINUED

PLTS objective: To extend your thinking and develop metacognition.

To help understand the way your brain works answer these questions 'yes' or 'no':

1. I organise facts and material well.
2. I work step by step.
3. I can be impatient.
4. I read instructions before starting.
5. I like to work things out on paper.
6. I like working on my own.
7. I like to make lists.
8. I can concentrate well.
9. I like reading.
10. I enjoy working with numbers.

> More 'yes' than 'no'? You may be more of a logical thinker.

Now answer these questions 'yes' or 'no':

11. I prefer variety and excitement.
12. I like to doodle a lot.
13. I love trying out new ideas.
14. I think of creative solutions.
15. I like new experiences.
16. I just try out ideas as I go along.
17. I prefer to flick through a magazine starting at the back.
18. I make decisions based on gut feelings.
19. I find it hard to concentrate quite often.
20. I prefer art to reading and Maths.

> More 'yes' than 'no'? You may be more of a creative thinker.
>
> If you have a fairly equal number of yes/no answers you are in the middle, which is an excellent place to be because you are using all of your brain for learning!

WHAT SORT OF THINKER ARE YOU? - CONTINUED

PLTS objective: To extend your thinking and develop metacognition.

LEARNING HEALTH CHECK

Using *all* of your brain can make you more clever, so once you know which way you tend to think watch out for these health warnings.

Top tips for whole brain learning:

- Be open to trying new approaches.
- Don't get bogged down in detail.
- Practice working well with others.
- Vary your learning styles and habits to keep your creative brain working.
- Don't forget details—one step at a time.
- Make yourself do some planning and prioritising in advance.
- Avoid procrastination (putting things off until the last minute!).
- Avoid distraction and distracting others.
- Don't rush in without thinking.
- Read instructions and check work when finished.
- Plan deadlines and check them out.

TASK

Think of a job or career you would like. How would you use your logical and creative thinking in this role?

Now decide which is the most useful.

What sort of careers do creative thinkers have?

What sort of careers do logical thinkers have?

What sort of career could you have if you were good at both?

HOW DID I DO?

Write a statement to describe yourself as a thinker. Think of one challenge to set yourself to grow your brain and record it in your Tracker Pack.

....

....

PUTTING YOUR PLTS INTO PRACTICE

ACTIVITY
11
PROJECT 1   5 HOURS

PLTS objective: Identify questions about learning, carry out research and communicate your learning.

GET EXCITED!

Fold your arms. Now fold them the other way. How does that feel?

Your brain enjoys doing things in certain comfortable ways. It also likes learning in its own way.

Each brain is very individual, like your thumbprint. However, if you understand and practice lots of ways to learn you will expand your brain power.

MAIN ACTIVITY

GROUP RESEARCH PROJECT

Find out more about learning styles so that you can grow your brain power. Get into groups and allocate roles and tasks, negotiate with your teacher a timeframe and deadline for this research task. Your task is to create a presentation about a chosen learning style or one of the Smarts to deliver to the group. You must also choose a piece of music to go with your presentation that inspires you to learn. Your presentation must include:

- Methods of learning.
- Activities that will help learning.
- Examples of famous people that demonstrate this learning style.
- Your chosen inspirational song.

PROJECT 1 – BRAIN BREAKTHROUGH
PUTTING YOUR PLTS INTO PRACTICE – CONTINUED

PLTS objective: Identify questions about learning, carry out research and communicate your learning.

As you listen to the presentations fill in a box like this for each group:

	What was good about it?	What constructive advice can you give to make it even better?	How well did you contribute to your group's effort?
Team 1			
Team 2			
Team 3			

How has your brain become smarter? Create a learning map that shows everything you now know about your brain. Then answer this quiz:

PUTTING YOUR PLTS
iNTO PRACTiCE - CONTiNUED

ACTIVITY
11
PROJECT 1   PAGE 3

PLTS objective: Identify questions about learning, carry out research and communicate your learning.

- What is your learning style?

....

- How can you become a better learner?

....

- Why do you need to be emotionally intelligent?

....

- How can you control your moods?

....

- Why does it help to think positively?

....

Write three targets to make your brain smarter.

1. ....

2. ....

3. ....

CREATE A LEARNiNG TREE

Trace around your hand onto coloured paper, cut it out and write down what you have learnt from project Brain Breakthrough on the hand. Stick your hand on the learning tree on the wall in the classroom.

Project 2
Fair Trade

WHAT iS FAiR?

ACTIVITY
1
PROJECT 2   2 HOURS

PLTS objective: Generating ideas, evaluating actions, research and questioning.

GET EXCiTED!

What do we mean by *fair trade*? 'Fair is foul and foul is fair' was chanted by the witches in *Macbeth*. What do you think it means? What do we mean by *fair*? Fair play ... Fair dos ... Fair enough ... Can you think of any other expressions that include *fair*?

MAiN ACTiViTY

1. Working in pairs, use a tick or cross to respond to these statements:

- It's not fair to steal. ☐

- If I hit you, it's fair for you to hit me. ☐

- I forgot my homework so it was fair that I had to stand in the corner for the rest of the lesson. ☐

- It was fair that the whole class got a detention because we were noisy. ☐

- If people bomb us, so it's only fair that we bomb them. ☐

- I helped at home with the washing up so it's only fair that I get some new trainers. ☐

- If I lived in a country where I was poor because I couldn't get a job, it would be fair for me to be able to come to a country where I could earn some money. ☐

- These statements are very fair. ☐

WHAT iS FAIR? - CONTiNUED

PLTS objective: Generating ideas, evaluating actions, research and questioning.

2. Now write lots of definitions of *fair*.

....

....

....

....

....

....

....

Finish these sentences:

i.   It's rained all summer so it's fair that

....

ii. I eat healthy food so it is not fair that

....

iii. I try to be kind to my sister but it's so unfair that she

....

Make up three more.

....

....

....

PROJECT 2 – FAIR TRADE

WHAT iS FAiR? – CONTiNUED

ACTIVITY
1
PROJECT 2 PAGE 3

PLTS objective: Generating ideas, evaluating actions, research and questioning.

3. Write three definitions of what *fair trade* might be.

....

....

....

4. Write three definitions of what *unfair trade* might be.

....

....

....

5. Now research on the internet or using books to check out your answers.

HOW DiD i DO?

Define *fair trade* and *unfair trade*.

....

....

How did you think, evaluate and question in this lesson?

....

....

How well have you worked with others?

....

....

....

....

	Rate your skills 1–5
Thinking	
Questioning and researching	
Evaluating	

38

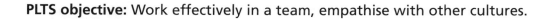

PROJECT 2 - FAIR TRADE

MARKET RESEARCH

ACTIVITY
2
PROJECT 2 · 2-3 HOURS

PLTS objective: Work effectively in a team, empathise with other cultures.

GET EXCITED!

Find out what other people know about fair trade. Do a word association game with the whole class that starts off with the word *fair*.

MAIN ACTIVITY

If the answer is, 'Yes, we have no bananas', what is the question? Discuss the difference between open and closed questions and their usefulness for surveys: How old are you? How are you old? Do you like bananas? What do you like about bananas? What makes a good question when you are a researcher?

Form a team to achieve the next task—appoint a team leader, timekeeper, notetaker, includer and listener. In your teams create ten questions for a questionnaire about fair trade. Conduct the survey on fair trade and gather your results. Analyse them. Present your findings to the class.

HOW DID I DO?

Did you find out what people think about fair trade and why?

How well did you perform in your team?

....

How well did your team perform and why?

....

How could your team improve?

....

PART 1 - PRODUCT RESEARCH

PLTS objective: To work successfully as part of a team, to manage information effectively, to demonstrate excellent communication skills.

GET EXCITED!

Create two or three newspaper headlines that show the power of successful teamwork, e.g. 'Gold medal for British rowing team' or 'Local village wins first prize in Britain in Bloom competition'.

....

....

....

What is your preferred role in a team?

My role is ....

and it will make the team work brilliantly if I ....

MAIN ACTIVITY

The objective of this exercise is to increase your knowledge about a fair trade product and meet your competency objectives. Get into the same teams formed for Activity 2. Choose a product to focus on (e.g. chocolate, bananas, flowers, coffee, tea, clothes, wine). Investigate your product. How is it farmed? How is it refined? How is it produced? How is it distributed?

Present your findings aimed at a young teen audience as either a leaflet, PowerPoint presentation, newspaper article, poster or mind-map. Your team will need to explain what you have done and what you have learnt throughout this process.

HOW DID I DO?

What did I do well in my team? ....

Even better if ....

PART 2 - ASSESSMENT OF OUTCOME

PLTS objective: To work successfully as part of a team, to manage information effectively, to demonstrate excellent communication skills.

GET EXCITED!

Make three positive comments from listening to other groups' presentations relating to the competency objective, reflecting on what excellent teamwork is and how to become a better team player.

 ## MAIN ACTIVITY

Praise and advice. As a group, write down *three good things* about each group presentation based on these headings:

Communication
Teamwork
Learning

Now write down *three pieces of advice* about each group presentation based on these headings:

Communication
Teamwork
Learning

PART 2 - ASSESSMENT OF OUTCOME

ACTIVITY 3
PROJECT 2 PAGE 2

PLTS objective: To work successfully as part of a team, to manage information effectively, to demonstrate excellent communication skills.

Now do the same for your own group:

Communication
Teamwork
Learning

Now do the same for yourself about your own performance and then discuss with the group:

Communication
Teamwork
Learning

HOW DID i DO?

What have you learnt from this lesson?

....

....

What makes groups work well?

....

....

How could your role have been better?

....

....

PROJECT 2 - FAiR TRADE
SPEND, SPEND, SPEND (1) - HOW THE GOVERNMENT SPENDS YOUR MONEY

PLTS objective: Researching and communicating information using ICT as a team.

GET EXCITED!

In pairs, imagine you are the Prime Minister and you had a million pounds to spend on this country. How would you spend it?

MAiN ACTiViTY

Who runs the finances for the country? What different types of taxes are there? Write a list of the things our taxes are spent on and put the list in order of priority.

Form your teams and decide on the roles for the next activity. You will need a team leader, timekeeper, notetaker, includer and listener.

As a group, decide how much you would spend on each of the sectors below. Divide the £557 billion pounds that the UK government spends based on your priorities.

	Sector	£billion
1		
2		
3		
4		
5		
6		
7		
8		
9		
10		
Total		557

43

PROJECT 2 – FAIR TRADE
SPEND, SPEND, SPEND (1) – HOW THE GOVERNMENT SPENDS YOUR MONEY – CONTINUED

PLTS objective: Researching and communicating information using ICT as a team.

There are ten sectors to choose from:

1. Social protection (unemployment benefit, pensions, child support, etc.)
2. Public services (recreation and leisure)
3. Housing and environment
4. Public order and safety
5. Industry, agriculture, employment and training
6. Defence
7. Education
8. Transport
9. Health (NHS)
10. Personal social services (social services, care of children, elderly, etc.)

SPEND, SPEND, SPEND (1) - HOW THE GOVERNMENT SPENDS YOUR MONEY - CONTINUED

PLTS objective: Researching and communicating information using ICT as a team.

HOW DID I DO?

How should government groups decide what to spend money on?

....

....

....

....

....

....

How well did you work in a team?

....

....

....

....

....

....

Better if

....

....

....

....

....

....

PROJECT 2 – FAIR TRADE
SPEND, SPEND, SPEND (2) – MAKING DECISIONS ABOUT MONEY

ACTIVITY 5

PROJECT 2 · 2 HOURS

PLTS objective: To reflect on how spending decisions are made and how this data can be communicated.

GET EXCITED!

Floods devastate the country and 100,000 people are affected. How much money will you give to help them?

MAIN ACTIVITY

1. In your groups review your spending decisions and create a report to deliver to a professional audience about the decisions you have made. Use a spreadsheet to handle data-performing equations and produce a graph or chart. Deliver your report to the class.

2. Compare your report with the way the money was spent by the government over the period of one year (see table below).

Sector	£billion
Social protection	161
Public services	59
Housing and environment	22
Public order and safety	33
Industry, etc.	21
Defence	32
Education	77
Transport	20
Health	104
Personal social services	28
Total	**557**

SPEND, SPEND, SPEND (2) - MAKING DECISIONS ABOUT MONEY - CONTINUED

PLTS objective: To reflect on how spending decisions are made and how this data can be communicated.

HOW DID I DO?

Write a short budget speech to justify your sector spending.

....

....

....

....

....

....

....

....

....

How well did I manage information using ICT?

....

....

....

....

How well did my group work?

....

....

....

....

iMPORT AND EXPORT

ACTIVITY
6
PROJECT 2   4 HOURS

PLTS objective: To communicate well as a team, to manage and present
information about importing and exporting products.

GET EXCiTED!

Think of three reasons why some countries are rich and some countries are poor.

1. ....

....

....

2. ....

....

....

3. ....

....

....

iMPORT AND EXPORT - CONTiNUED

PLTS objective: To communicate well as a team, to manage and present information about importing and exporting products.

MAiN ACTiViTY

Which products do we import? Tick the correct box (some may be both!).

Produced	Home-produced	Imported
Bananas		
Pineapples		
Tea		
Coffee		
Chocolate		
Oil		
Rice		
Potatoes		
Apples		
Computers		

1. Look at your list of imported products. Which countries do they come from?

....

....

....

....

....

....

....

....

....

PLTS objective: To communicate well as a team, to manage and present
information about importing and exporting products.

2. What makes a country rich?

....

....

....

3. What makes a country poor?

....

....

....

4. If we couldn't import *any* products from other countries because of climate change, how
would it affect you?

....

....

....

Now think about countries which are not as rich as the UK and consider why. Assign group
members their roles again (see Activity 2). Your group task is to:

• research/discuss why some countries have a debt

• research what we mean by third world debt

• find out about how countries pay interest on that debt

• present a campaign using leaflets, posters or PowerPoint presentations arguing for and
against the campaign to drop third world debt.

CREATE YOUR OWN PRODUCT

ACTIVITY 7 PROJECT 2 2 HOURS

PLTS objective: Take part in a team and contribute to the development of a product, generate ideas, plan time and resources effectively.

GET EXCITED!

What fair trade products do you use/eat? Where do they come from?

MAIN ACTIVITY

Assign the team roles (see Activity 2) and complete the following tasks: create a fair trade product using fair trade ingredients or produce (e.g. cookies, jewellery, clothes, smoothies, sweets) then create a marketing campaign.

HOW DID I DO?

How is our product fair trade?

....

....

How did we work together as a team?

....

....

51

PROJECT 2 - FAIR TRADE
TAKE YOUR PRODUCT TO MARKET

ACTIVITY
8
PROJECT 2   5 HOURS

PLTS objective: Evaluate your own and others' work, communicate and collaborate effectively with others.

GET EXCITED!

Think of a single sentence to say why your team worked the best in the previous lesson.

....

MAIN ACTIVITY

Create a fair trade stall for your team to sell your products. Visit other stalls and see which products you would like to buy.

As a follow up to the fair, the team should choose from the following activities:

1. Write a letter to the Prime Minister telling him about fair trade.

2. Produce an information leaflet for your product.

3. Create a PowerPoint presentation about fair trade.

4. Produce a newspaper article or newsletter reporting on the outcomes of the fair trade project for primary school children.

5. Write to a local supermarket giving reasons why they should stock fair trade produce.

HOW DID I DO?

Evaluate one team's product at the fair.

....

....

State what they did well and why it was effective.

....

....

State what they could have improved and how.

....

....

PROJECT 2 – FAIR TRADE

HOW DID WE ALL DO?

PLTS objective: Self- and peer-assessment.

ACTIVITY
9
PROJECT 2 · 1 HOUR

GET EXCITED!

What qualities would make the best fair trade product out of all those you have seen?

....

....

....

....

....

MAIN ACTIVITY

Each group reminds the class of the name and slogan of their product.

PRAISE AND ADVICE

Write a praise comment on each of the following headings for each group.

	Insert a grade from 1–5 and add a comment
Learning about fair trade	
Communicating ideas	
Teamwork	

Write an advice comment on each of these headings for each group:

	Insert a grade from 1–5 and add a comment
Learning about fair trade	
Communicating ideas	
Teamwork	

53

HOW DID WE ALL DO?
– CONTINUED

ACTIVITY
9
PROJECT 2 PAGE 2

PLTS objective: Self- and peer-assessment.

Write a praise comment on each of these for your own group:

	Insert a grade from 1–5 and add a comment
Learning about fair trade	
Communicating ideas	
Teamwork	

Write an advice comment on each of these for your own group:

	Insert a grade from 1–5 and add a comment
Learning about fair trade	
Communicating ideas	
Teamwork	

PLTS objective: Self- and peer-assessment.

Now fill in the boxes for your own performance.

Praise:

	Insert a grade from 1–5 and add a comment
Learning about fair trade	
Communicating ideas	
Teamwork	

Advice:

	Insert a grade from 1–5 and add a comment
Learning about fair trade	
Communicating ideas	
Teamwork	

HOW DID I DO?

Say one thing you have learnt about yourself as a member of the team.

....

....

Say one thing you are going to do differently as a result of the fair trade project.

....

....

Project 3
Money, Money, Money

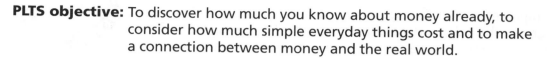

PROJECT 3 – MONEY, MONEY, MONEY

THE COST OF LIVING

ACTIVITY
1
PROJECT 3   1 HOUR

PLTS objective: To discover how much you know about money already, to consider how much simple everyday things cost and to make a connection between money and the real world.

GET EXCITED!

How much income do you have each week? Create a learning map of what you spend it on.

MAIN ACTIVITY

1. Money word wall display. See which of these terms you understand. Write associated words and images around each word for the wall display: credit, tax, wages, insurance, mortgage, currency, pension, loan, store card, interest, savings.

2. Money quiz. Estimate to the nearest amount—choosing from the box below.

   1. What is the minimum wage per hour?
   2. What is the single person's old age state pension per week?
   3. How much is family allowance for the first child per week?
   4. How much is the Education Maintenance Allowance that students get post-16 worth per week?
   5. How much does a passport cost?
   6. How much does the cheapest mobile phone cost?
   7. How much is a first class stamp?

Choose answers from this list:

   £5
   £60
   £25
   £28
   £30
   £80
   50p

3. Name three songs that have lyrics related to money.

1. ....

2. ....

3. ....

PROJECT 3 – MONEY, MONEY, MONEY
PLANNING BUDGETS

PLTS objective: To improve your knowledge of how to manage your own money, to undertake independent research about what items cost and to cooperate with others acting as a team member or team leader.

GET EXCITED!

You save £5 a week for ten weeks. In one minute plan what you will spend it on.

MAIN ACTIVITY

In groups of four or five carry out the tasks below. Create a hypothesis … guess which will cost the most! Rank order them in terms of the most and least expensive.

Plan a budget for the following by finding out what the costs are and writing a list of what you will spend in your teams. You will need to research from catalogues and the internet to find out the prices for things. Make a list of everything you think you will need and price them up. Add up your total for the challenge and then present your budgets to the class.

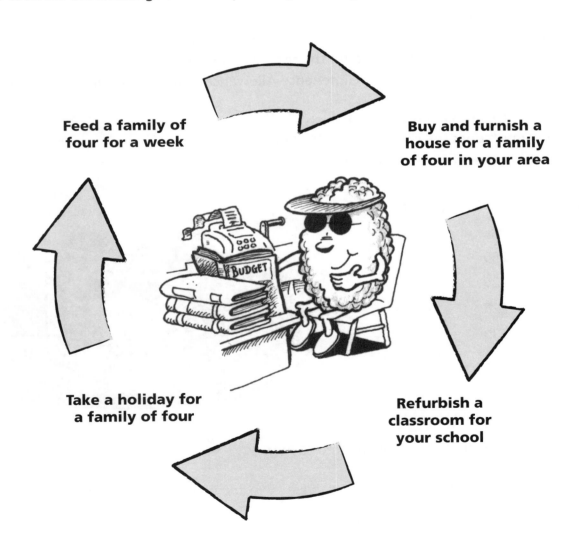

Feed a family of four for a week

Buy and furnish a house for a family of four in your area

Take a holiday for a family of four

Refurbish a classroom for your school

58

PLANNING BUDGETS
- CONTINUED

PLTS objective: To improve your knowledge of how to manage your own money, to undertake independent research about what items cost and to cooperate with others acting as a team member or team leader.

Feed a family of four for a week	Cost
....	....
....	....
....	....
....	....
....	....
....	....
....	....
....	....

Buy and furnish a house for a family of four in your area	Cost
....	....
....	....
....	....
....	....
....	....
....	....
....	....

Take a holiday for a family of four	Cost
....	....
....	....
....	....
....	....
....	....
....	....
....	....

Refurbish a classroom for your school	Cost
....	....
....	....
....	....
....	....
....	....
....	....
....	....

HOW DID I DO?

How could you make each of these a bit cheaper or more expensive?

PROJECT 3 – MONEY, MONEY, MONEY

iS MONEY GOOD OR EVIL?

ACTIVITY
3
PROJECT 3 1-2 HOURS

PLTS objective: To reflect on why we consider being rich important, to listen to each other and respond with empathy and to ask appropriate questions at a higher level.

GET EXCITED!

What is the Rich List? Name some very rich people that you know and write what they do on a Post-it note.

MAIN ACTIVITY

Read the parable of the talents from the Bible (Matthew 25: 14–30). Discuss in pairs a question that results from your discussion of that story. Each pair should write their question on the board. The class then chooses the question they wish to investigate in a Community of Enquiry. In a circle all students must discuss the chosen question and give their opinion or ask further questions.

COMMUNiTY OF ENQUiRY

Further questions for discussion in the enquiry:

* Does being rich make you happy?
* How does being rich make you happy?
* What else do you need to make you happy?
* How can being rich make you unhappy?
* If you won a million pounds how could it make you unhappy?
* Why don't animals need money?

HOW DiD i DO?

Make a list of what would become important if money became worthless.

....

....

....

....

....

....

60

PROJECT 3 - MONEY, MONEY, MONEY
CREATE A CURRENCY

PLTS objective: You will research from a range of sources about currencies and participate in a scheme of rewards using your chosen class currency. You will work as part of a team to create your own currency design.

GET EXCITED!

Name as many currencies as you can think of and find out their exchange rate against the British pound.

Currency	Exchange Rate

MAIN ACTIVITY

In teams research the history of money and various currencies. Design your own currency—create a name for it, design a note and coins and create prototypes. Find some products and price them up in your currency.

Each group then chooses their favourite currency which then becomes the class currency. Fifty notes are produced and given out for jobs around the group (e.g. litter collection, display checking, giving out books, helping each other). The notes can be cashed in at the end of term for prizes or real money.

61

MANAGE YOUR MONEY

ACTIVITY
5
PROJECT 3   1-2 HOURS

PLTS objective: To understand your attitude to money, to reflect on how you can make money work well for you, to review the financial vocabulary with reference to your own money profile and to set yourself targets for developing your skills.

GET EXCITED!

Write down the three things that you most like to spend money on.

....

....

....

 ## MAIN ACTIVITY

What is your money personality—spender, saver or 'spaver'? Answer the questions in the pound and penny profile as honestly as you can. Tick the boxes that most apply to you:

Do you work for any of your income?	No	Sometimes	Yes
What is your total weekly income?	£0–5	£6–20	£21+
How much do you spend each week?	£21+	£6–20	£0–5
How much have you got in savings?	£0–10	£11–100	£100+
How often do you go shopping for yourself?	Once or more per week	Two or three times per month	Once a month
If you want something can you save up for it?	Never	Sometimes	Always

MANAGE YOUR MONEY - CONTINUED

ACTIVITY
5
PROJECT 3 PAGE 2

PLTS objective: To understand your attitude to money, to reflect on how you can make money work well for you, to review the financial vocabulary with reference to your own money profile and to set yourself targets for developing your skills.

How much do you spend on clothes each month?	£50+	£11–50	£0–5
How much do you spend on music/multimedia each month?	£11+	£6–10	£0–5
How much do you spend going out each week?	£11+	£6–10	£0–5
How much do you spend on food and drink each week?	£11+	£6–10	£0–5
Have you ever borrowed any money?	Often	Sometimes	Rarely
Do you pay back your borrowings?	Sometimes	Yes—eventually	Yes
What would you do if you were given £100?	Spend it straight away on stuff I want	Spend some and save some	Put it in a savings account
What would you do if you won a million pounds?	Buy a house, a car and have an expensive holiday	Go on a shopping spree, give some to charity and put the rest in a bank	Get advice from a financial advisor
Add up the ticks in each column			
Do you think you are a spender, saver or spaver (a bit of each)?	Spender	Spaver	Saver

Is this what you thought you would be? Set some targets for the future so that you can manage your budget.

PROJECT 3 – MONEY, MONEY, MONEY
MANAGE YOUR MONEY – CONTINUED

ACTIVITY 5 PROJECT 3 PAGE 3

PLTS objective: To understand your attitude to money, to reflect on how you can make money work well for you, to review the financial vocabulary with reference to your own money profile and to set yourself targets for developing your skills.

REVIEW

Fill in the financial pros and cons table with everything you know or can find out about these topics and how they relate to *your* profile:

	PROS	CONS
Credit card		
Debit card		
Pension		
Mortgage for a house		
Renting a house		
Store card		
eBay purchases		
Bank account		
Income tax		
Internet shopping		
Loans		
Pawn shop		
Insurance		
Catalogue shopping		

Discuss each of these as a class and then prioritise them.

PROJECT 3 – MONEY, MONEY, MONEY
ADVERTISING – CREATING A NEED OR FEEDING A GREED?

PLTS objective: You will understand the codes and conventions of advertising and how it impacts on the target audience. You will develop creative ideas that will help people manage money effectively. You will review your learning and progress in this project.

GET EXCITED!

Look at a magazine or recall TV adverts that feed on our emotions and create a need for expensive items.

MAIN ACTIVITY

Analyse one magazine and choose ten adverts. Look at the prices of the products and find out or estimate what they may cost to manufacture. Looking at your pound and penny profile (see Activity 5) which products tempt you? What techniques are used to make us want expensive items such as cars, make-up, clothes and so on?

....

....

....

....

....

....

HOW DID I DO

In your team create one of the following to demonstrate what you have learnt from this project: (1) an advice website about money, (2) a leaflet for primary school children helping them to learn the essentials about money or (3) prepare a one-hour lesson for Year 6 students about money.

Project 4
Saving Planet Earth

A STORY FOR THE FUTURE

PLTS objective: By the end of this activity you will participate in a group reading of a text and reflect on the messages the text contains.

ACTIVITY
1
PROJECT 4   2 HOURS

MAIN ACTIVITY

As a group read *A Sound of Thunder* by Ray Bradbury. This is a science fiction short story about people travelling backwards in time and breaking the rules. This scary story shows us how our unthinking actions can change the world. Following on from this story:

What are we doing to our planet now that could impact on our great-great-grandchildren's lives? Write a list of everything you can think of and what its impact may be in the future.

What actions are we taking that may damage the future?

....

....

....

....

....

....

....

What could happen in the future?

....

....

....

....

....

....

....

WHAT ARE THE PROBLEMS?

PLTS objective: You will practise working effectively in a team to carry out research into the various problems facing planet Earth.

GET EXCITED!

In pairs write three things you love about living on this planet compared to what it might be like to live on the moon.

....

....

....

....

....

MAIN ACTIVITY

In your group use the six focus cards (below) to plan research on your topic and prepare a five-minute presentation for the class to inform them about the facts and debates on your particular focus.

---

1. The energy gap

'150 experts say more nuclear power needed'

'In 2015 energy demand will exceed supply by 23% in UK'

'WWF says UK does not need nuclear power as we can't get rid of the waste'

'Oil to run out by 2100'

Key words
Fossil fuels
Combustion
Carbon dioxide
Sustainable/unsustainable
Renewable/non-renewable energy
Solar energy
Biomass energy
Wind energy
Tidal energy
Nuclear energy
Gigawatt
Energy saving/conservation

2. Nature under threat

'Pandas or people?'

'25% of land animals and plants to be extinct by 2050'

'Fen orchid to disappear—who cares?'

'Humans are causing the greatest mass extinction since the death of the dinosaurs'

Key words
Extinction
Conservation
Species
Habitat loss
Food chains and webs
Endangered
Red List
Adapt
Biodiversity
Ecosystem
Deforestation
Desertification

WHAT ARE THE PROBLEMS?
– CONTINUED

PLTS objective: You will practise working effectively in a team to carry out research into the various problems facing planet Earth.

---

3. Extreme weather

'Southern Europe to become a desert'
'Gulf Stream may stop—Britain to freeze'
'By 2100 the Earth could be warmer than for the last 10 million years'
'London to flood'

Key words
Carbon dioxide
Methane
Global warming
Climate change
Gulf Stream
Polar ice
Floods
Storms
Hurricanes
Typhoons
Monsoons
Drought
Desertification
Sea level rise

4. Poisoning the Planet

'The average American makes 20.4 tonnes of carbon dioxide but China makes the most'
'In some cities breathing the air is like smoking 20 cigarettes a day'
'900,000 tonnes of oil/year spilled into the oceans'

Key words
Carbon dioxide
Methane
Landfill
Pollution
Non-biodegradable
Toxic waste
Heavy metals
Litter
Chlorofluorocarbons (CFCs)
Acid rain
Industrialisation
Sewage
Asbestos
Carbon footprint
Food miles

WHAT ARE THE PROBLEMS?
- CONTINUED

ACTIVITY
2
PROJECT 4   PAGE 3

PLTS objective: You will practise working effectively in a team to carry out research into the various problems facing planet Earth.

5. Waste and recycling

'Think globally, act locally'
'We would need 3.5 Earths if we all lived like Americans'
'Consumer societies are happier'
'Reduce, reuse, recycle'

Key words

Landfill
Metals
Glass
Plastics
Paper
Water
Composting
Conservation
Reforestation
Energy conservation
Food waste
Carbon footprint
Consumer culture
Exporting waste
Packaging

6. Over-population of the planet

'World population to rise by 50% in 40 years'
'China limits number of children'
'Large families are happy families'
'Three billion people live on less than 50p per day'

Key words

Birth rate
Death rate
Billions
Developed/developing countries
Poverty
Demographic change
Birth laws
Growth of cities/urbanisation
Consumerism
Limited resources
Food
Water
Famine
Energy demand
Resource wars

PROJECT 4 - SAVING PLANET EARTH
WHAT ARE THE PROBLEMS?
- CONTINUED

ACTIVITY
2
PROJECT 2 PAGE 4

PLTS objective: You will practise working effectively in a team to carry out research into the various problems facing planet Earth.

Typing the key words above into an internet search engine should produce lots of useful hits but also try these websites:

http://www.recyclenow.org
http://www. recycling-guide.org.uk
http://www.stopglobalwarming.org
http://tiki.oneworld.net
http://www.bbc.co.uk/climate
http://www.bbc.co.uk/nature/animals/conservation
http://www.direct.gov.uk/environmentandgreenerliving

PRAISE AND ADVICE

Write a positive statement about each of the presentations and some advice about how it could be even better. Write three good things about your own work or presentation and write one thing that could have been better and say how.

....

....

....

....

....

....

....

....

....

....

....

....

....

....

WHAT ARE THE SOLUTIONS?

ACTIVITY
3
PROJECT 4   3-5 HOURS

PLTS objective: You will use your creative thinking skills to consider how we can address the concerns about our planet and effectively participate in making a persuasive case for action after assessing all viewpoints.

GET EXCITED!

Think of three reasons why *you* should find some solutions to these problems.

1. ....

2. ....

3. ....

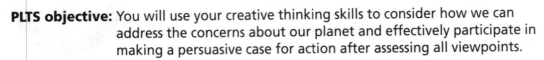

MAIN ACTIVITY

Choose one of the following to complete in pairs:

Present a case for limiting the birth rate to one child per family

Create an advertising campaign called 'How can we stop the lights going out?'

Make a scary weather survival pack

PLANET EARTH SOLUTIONS

Produce a leaflet showing how you can reduce your carbon footprint

Produce a website called 'Which animals shall we save and how?'

Create an eco-home – a drawing or model

PROJECT 4 - SAVING PLANET EARTH
GET PRACTICAL TO SAVE THE PLANET

PLTS objective: You will reflect on what you have researched about eco-issues. You will develop your teamworking skills in a creative project by putting together a case to persuade others to care for our planet.

GET EXCITED!

Our emotional brains love colour, rhythm, rhyme, humour, novelty, stories, challenge, love and relevance. How can we persuade people to save the planet using these techniques?

MAIN ACTIVITY

In groups choose to create one of the following that will have a powerful impact on others:

- Create a recycled sculpture.
- Write a rap to save the future.
- Perform a drama of life in 2070.
- Use a digital camera to create a PowerPoint presentation of the threat to our planet.
- Create masks and perform a mime.
- Write a poem or story called 'Save the planet'.

Before you start write down the success criteria for your chosen activity. How will you know it's good?

Chosen activity	Success criteria

PROJECT 4 - SAVING PLANET EARTH
GET PRACTICAL TO
SAVE THE PLANET - CONTINUED

PLTS objective: You will reflect on what you have researched about eco-issues. You will develop your teamworking skills in a creative project by putting together a case to persuade others to care for our planet.

Demonstrate what you have created to other classes and ask them to evaluate its impact on their awareness of issues relating to Saving Planet Earth.

Score each others' efforts according to how much creativity they have used and how much it makes you think about the problems.

Peer-assessment sheet (mark out of 5)

	It made me think about the planet	All team members took part	It was explained clearly	It demon-strated creative thinking	Total score
Team 1					
Team 2					
Team 3					

PROJECT 4 - SAVING PLANET EARTH
GET PRACTICAL TO
SAVE THE PLANET - CONTINUED

PLTS objective: You will reflect on what you have researched about eco-issues. You will develop your teamworking skills in a creative project by putting together a case to persuade others to care for our planet.

	It made me think about the planet	All team members took part	It was explained clearly	It demon-strated creative thinking	Total score
Team 4					
Team 5					

Now complete your Tracker Pack for your own PLTS progress.

75

Tracker Pack

TRACKER PACK - PAGE 1

USING THE PLTS TO BECOME A GOLDEN LEARNER

What are we looking for? For each of the competences you can mark a cross where you think you have performed for this project or lesson (you can add the date too and your initials).

Personal skills (P)		Write your P targets here:
Team workers *Young people work confidently with others, adapting to different contexts and taking responsibility for their own part. They listen and value different views, resolving issues and creating sustainable relationships.*	**Team workers** I can work in a team to achieve common goals. I can compromise with others in my group. I can adapt to play many different roles in a group. I can show kindness to team players. I can take responsibility and I am confident in my contribution. I can give feedback to other team members and groups.	
Effective participators *Young people who actively engage with issues that affect them and those around them. They play a full part in their school, college, workplace or community and take responsible action to improve life for everyone.*	**Effective participators** I can willingly take part and change issues that affect our lives. I can make a persuasive case for action. I can listen to other viewpoints and work as a negotiator to reach workable solutions. I know that people have different ethics and these should be respected. I understand that being a good citizen involves helping the community.	
Learning (L)		Write your L targets here:
Self-managers *Young people who organise themselves, showing personal responsibility, initiative, creativity and enterprise with a commitment to learning and self-improvement.*	**Reflective Learners** I can assess others and myself and can give positive feedback. I can set my own goals and targets. I can analyse my work and improve it. I can accept positive and negative feedback. I can improve on my mistakes for future progress. I can confidently present my work in front of an audience.	

Learning (L) *cntd*		Write your L targets here:
Reflective learners *Young people can evaluate their strengths and limitations and set themselves realistic goals with criteria for success. They monitor their own performance and progress, inviting feedback and adapting their learning effectively.*	**Self-managers** I seek out challenges and new responsibilities. I react well to changing the plan that I have made. I keep going when the going gets tough. I can deal with pressure and deadlines then seek help when I need it. I can set myself targets and work towards them. I show initiative and take risks.	
Thinking (T) **Independent enquirers** *Young people who can process and evaluate information in their investigations, planning what to do and how to go about it. They recognise others have different beliefs and attitudes.*	**Independent learners** I can plan and do research, taking into consideration the consequences of my decision. I can think deeply about a subject, putting myself in other people's shoes. I can look at and write about information, deciding how important it is. I can take into consideration different beliefs and feelings when making decisions. I back up my ideas with thought about arguments and evidence.	Write your T targets here:

Thinking (T) cntd		
Creative thinkers *Young people think creatively by generating and exploring ideas and making original connections. They try different ways to tackle a problem, working with others to find imaginative solutions.*	**Creative thinkers** I can come up with ideas and explore other possibilities. I can ask questions about a topic to make me think in more depth. I can combine mine and other people's ideas and past experiences to compromise, where needed, and think of new ideas as a result. I can question whether assumptions we make are accurate. I try out new ways of solving problems and pursue ideas. I can change/compromise ideas to fit new circumstances.	Write your L targets here:

PERSONAL SKILLS - HOW DiD i DO?

For each of the competences you can mark a cross where you think you have performed for this project or activity (you can add the date too and your initials).

PLTS assessment

PLTS – typical traits	Bronze	Silver	Gold
Personal skills • Team workers • Effective participators	'I find it hard to get on with others' 'I only want to work with my friends' 'I don't really care about other people in the world' 'I lose my temper easily'	'I like working in groups' 'I listen to other people's opinions' 'I care about the rest of the world' 'I want to do the right thing' 'I take part in a club at school' 'I want to work hard and do well in the future' 'I am interested in the news'	'My aim is that our group does well on the project' 'I think a lot about how I can help solve issues in the world' 'I have volunteered to help out in my community' 'I have a variety of hobbies and interests' 'I am always thinking of ideas and projects' 'I know just what I want to be in the future—even if it changes each week!' 'People get on with me and I know how to get on with all sorts of different people' 'I believe I can do anything I set my mind on and most of all I want to help other people'

Praise:...

Advice: ....

Targets: ....

LEARNING SKILLS - HOW DID i DO?

For each of the competences you can mark a cross where you think you have performed for this project or activity. You can add the date too and your initials.

Me:

Teacher:

PLTS – typical traits	Bronze	Silver	Gold
Learning skills • Self-managers • Reflective learners	'I am a kinaesthetic learner so get bored listening' 'I only work when I am interested' 'I rarely finish my work' 'I can't see the point in learning'	'I am learning to use my brain in various ways' 'Making mistakes is an important part of learning' 'I make lists of things I have to do' 'I think carefully when I work out how to improve my work' 'I know learning means hard work and lots of practice'	'I believe I can learn to be more clever if I work hard enough' 'I really learn from making mistakes' 'I like a challenge as it makes me learn more' 'I always have a plan' 'I believe I can do anything if I try hard enough' 'I am growing my brain through extending my learning styles' 'I like getting feedback about how I am doing so that I can improve' 'If something doesn't work then I try a different way, then a different way until it works' 'I am able to draft and re-draft my work until it is right'

Praise:...

Advice: ....

Targets: ....

THINKING SKILLS - HOW DID I DO?

For each of the competences you can mark a cross where you think you have performed for this project or activity (you can add the date too and your initials).

PLTS – typical traits	Bronze	Silver	Gold
Thinking skills • Independent enquirers • Creative thinkers	'I don't like thinking too much' 'I prefer to be told what to do' 'I can't think of ideas easily' 'I can't do it' 'I can't see how to do it' 'I can't be bothered' 'I don't like to be different'	'I like to work on my own sometimes' 'I can think of ideas and get others to help me' 'I will ask questions to help me with my work' 'I enjoy new situations and meeting new people' 'I can work well on my own'	'I always have lots of ideas' 'I like to work out why as well as how' 'I get on with my work and often do things that the teacher didn't ask for' 'I get very involved in my projects and usually go off in new directions' 'I like asking difficult questions' 'There is no limit to how much I can learn' 'I have my own individual style' 'I like to try many different solutions until I get it right' 'I like to know how things work for myself'

Praise: ....

Advice: ....

Targets: ....

PLTS PROGRESSION SUMMARY SHEET (SAMPLE)

	Activity 1	Activity 2	Activity 3	Activity 4	Activity 5	Activity 6	End of year summary
Personal skills (P)	Bronze	Silver	Silver	Gold	Silver	Gold	**Silver+**
Learning skills (L)	Silver	Bronze	Gold	Gold	Silver	Gold	**Gold-**
Thinking skills (T)	Bronze	Bronze	Bronze	Silver	Silver	Silver	**Bronze+**
PLTS summary	**Bronze+**	**Bronze+**	**Silver**	**Gold-**	**Silver**	**Gold-**	**Silver**

Note: Numbers or letters can be substituted if statistical data is required.

NOTES

84

NOTES

NOTES

NOTES

♛

Crown House Publishing Limited
www.crownhouse.co.uk – www.crownhousepublishing.com

Illustration Les Evans

ISBN 978-184590

9 781845 903